# THE SCOTTISH REGION IN THE 1970s AND 1980s

Andy Gibbs

*Front cover above*: With the Isle of Skye in the background and steam billowing from the train heating, an unidentified Class 26 waits to depart from Kyle of Lochalsh with a train for Inverness in June 1983.

*Front cover below*: Refurbished Class 101 set No. 102 curves onto the Tay Bridge at Wormit on 5 August 1977. Dundee can be seen on the opposite bank of the river. (S. Clark)

*Back cover*: In bright winter sunlight No. 26030 crosses the River Ness at Inverness with 2N20, the 11.08 from Kyle of Lochalsh, on 4 November 1981. (A. Gibbs)

First published 2020

Amberley Publishing
The Hill, Stroud
Gloucestershire, GL5 4EP

www.amberley-books.com



ISBN 978 1 4456 8189 4 (print)
ISBN 978 1 4456 8190 0 (ebook)



British Library Cataloguing in Publication Data.
A catalogue record for this book is available from the British Library.

Origination by Amberley Publishing.
Printed in the UK.

# Introduction

Welcome to the fifth of my regional photo albums. This volume will take you through the former Scottish Region of British Rail during the 1970s and 1980s – basically anything north of Carlisle and Berwick!

Spotting trains in Scotland was not going to happen very often as I lived in Brighton. You might see the odd Scottish Class 47 down south but nothing more exotic than that. It wasn't until a camping trip with the Venture Scouts got me to Ayr and Edinburgh and the weird and wonderful Scottish railways, or so they seemed to me.

Later, when I started work for British Rail, my first blue free passes were for mammoth trips from Falmer to Kyle of Lochalsh and a further trip to Thurso. I was a member of the Brighton Model Railway Club and we had decided to build a model of Kyle – any excuse for a trip north!

One of the perks of working for BR was reduced rates at the British Transport Hotel chain and this allowed me a couple of nights in Inverness and some photos around the area. Reduced rate holidays through another BR subsidiary, Golden Rail, meant a couple of consecutive years' summer holidays were weeks in Scotland, one based at Stirling and the other at Inverkip near Wemyss Bay.

The book is about a time when the trains were blue and grey and you could get a Sleeper from Glasgow and Edinburgh to Inverness and Haggis and chips for lunch in a Woolworths restaurant – delicious.

This is my record of those trips and others augmented by photos from my collection. A big thanks to Sandy Clark for supplying a lot of excellent images for the book too. We will start our journey on the west coast, heading through Glasgow and the West Highland line before returning to the east coast and heading for the far north via Aberdeen and Inverness.

Most of the images are scanned from 35 mm transparencies; there are also some images from medium format black and white negatives and slides too.

Doing the research for these series of books has been half the fun. Points of reference have included the *Rail Atlas of Britain* by Stuart Baker; my 1979 edition is extremely battered. Google Maps must think I have a very strange search pattern when trying to check locations. A lot has changed in the past thirty or so years.

A big thank you once again to the numerous railway websites that are a labour of love, 'keeping the gen alive', such as Rail Gen Archive, The Bashing Years, Class 40 Motherlist and The Chronicles of Napier, to name but a few. In addition to this there are various working timetables and the 1Hxx series of books, which have been used in the research for this and my other books.

When I've got to the end of each book, I've enjoyed a nice glass of beer from each area: Harvey's Armada for the Southern, Proper Job for the Western and Pedigree for the Midlands. For the Scottish Region, it's Lia Fail amber ale from the Inveralmond brewery. A very nice beer indeed. Enjoy!

At Floriston, between Carlisle and Gretna, we find No. 86244 heading south with an Intercity service bound for Euston on 16 July 1977. (S. Clark)

Heading north at Floriston, No. 40011 has an unidentified train of Mk 1 coaches in tow on 16 July 1977. This could be a Carlisle to Glasgow via Dumfries service. (S. Clark)

No mistaking the number on this loco. No. 47442 is captured working a northbound local service at Dumfries station on 2 May 1986. Some of the coaches are now sporting Scotrail logos.

No. 47410 heads south with a Glasgow Central to Nottingham service, seen here at Kilmarnock station in 1977. (A. Gibbs)

Just outside of Ayr station on 19 May 1979 we find No. 25191 with a train of parcels vans, formed of examples of BR and former LMS and SR vehicles. (S. Clark)

In a cloud of exhaust, a pair of Swindon-built three-car Class 126 DMUs accelerate away from Ayr bound for Glasgow Central on 19 May 1979. No. 25235 can also be seen in the depot. (S. Clark)

A line-up of three locomotives at Ayr Depot on 19 May 1979: Nos 27038, 25246 and 25235. (S. Clark)

No. 47617 *University of Stirling* arrives at Ayr with 1A04, the 14.25 Stranraer Harbour to Glasgow Central service, in September 1987. The old lady gets ready to jot the number down.

Kilwinning and it's a fine summer day as a Class 107/101 combination, No. 107427, arrives on a service to Largs in July 1984. (A. Gibbs)

A deserted Ardrossan Harbour sees a lonely Class 107 DMU waiting for passengers. (D. Burton)

On a lovely sunny day, No. 87034 *William Shakespeare* departs from Carstairs station with a southbound Intercity service on 26 July 1978. (S. Clark)

Four AC electric locos await their next turn of duty at Carstairs on 26 July 1978. From left to right: Nos 86021, 86023, 86248 and 84006. (S. Clark)

No. 40031 is captured at Carstairs with a train of sheeted hopper wagons on 26 July 1978. (S. Clark)

No. 47051 curves into Carstairs with 1C92, the 13.22 from Edinburgh Waverley, on 30 July 1979. This attaches at Carstairs to 1V95, the 13.35 from Glasgow Central, for the long run south to Taunton. No. 87027 *Wolf of Badendoch* can be seen in the distance. (S. Clark)

Class 86/0 No. 86029 powers through Carstairs with an unidentified northbound service formed of Mk 1 stock on 30 July 1979. (S. Clark)

It's a cold March day at Carstairs. Nos 27202 and 20131 can be seen 'on shed' on 24 March 1979. (S. Clark)

Under the mass of overhead line cables at Carstairs, HST set No. 254017 with power car No. 43089 trailing swings onto the line for Edinburgh on 30 June 1979. (S. Clark)

Carstairs station sees Class 20 No. 20123 shunting a train of engineers' wagons loaded with concrete troughing on 4 July 1981. (S. Clark)

Class 85 electric No. 85037 arrives at Carstairs with 1M47, the 17.20 Glasgow Central to Birmingham New Street on 15 June 1984. Additional coaches from Edinburgh, which departed at 17.10 as 1C94, are attached here.

Unusually with bonnets outermost, 'Choppers' Nos 20067 and 20100 trundle through Motherwell with a couple of brake vans in tow in July 1984. (A. Gibbs)

No. 86211 *City of Milton Keynes* arrives at Motherwell in July 1984 with 1S59, the 09.30 Euston to Inverness, 'The Clansman'. The electric loco will be detached in Mossend Yard and exchanged for a diesel loco to take the train through the Highlands. (A. Gibbs)

The crew lean out of the cab of No. 83002 as it passes through Motherwell with a Euston to Inverness Motorail working on 7 August 1982. I'm not sure what is amiss.

Nos 20149 and 20221 chirp through Motherwell with a train of tank wagons in July 1984. (A. Gibbs)

No. 87024 *Lord of the Isles* waits to depart from Motherwell with a southbound Intercity working in July 1984. An SNP poster can be seen on the bridge above. How times have changed! (A. Gibbs)

We move a little closer to Glasgow at Newton. Here we find Nos 303079 and 311096. The bunker-like signal box dominates the station. (S. Clark)

An unidentified Class 86/0 passes through Newton with a long train of empty Cartic4 wagons on 31 July 1981. (S. Clark)

Near to Rutherglen we find this unidentified Class 85 heading south with an Intercity service. (S. Clark)

Bridgeton and No. 303004, with Greater Glasgow logos, waits to depart back to Dalmuir Park amid the rubbish-strewn tracks on 9 April 1979. This contrasts nicely with the next photo. (S. Clark)

We move on five years and Nos 303010 and 314208, sporting Strathclyde Transport livery, certainly brighten up Bridgeton station on 15 June 1984.

Captured at Baileston, No. 26011 scurries along with a train of 16-ton mineral wagons on 2 June 1977. (S. Clark)

At Bedlay colliery near Annathill, we find Class 20 No. 20119 with a long train of 16-ton mineral wagons, loaded with coal, appearing out of the mist. (S. Clark)

No. 20119 once again, with the same train near to Bedlay colliery. The gloomy surroundings emphasise the scene. (S. Clark)

Class 86 No. 86228 *Vulcan Heritage* lays over at Glasgow Central after having brought in an ECS working on 13 February 1986. This will form a service to Euston.

No. 47404 *Hadrian* with a Glasgow Central to Stranraer service formed of the garishly painted Sealink-liveried Mk 1 coaches in September 1984.

With extremely battered paintwork, No. 86231 *Starlight Express* heads up an unidentified cross-country service at Glasgow Central on 28 May 1989. (P. Barber)

No. 20123 is on station pilot duty at Glasgow Central today and is about to head off to Polmadie with a recently arrived service from Euston in 1984. (A. Gibbs)

No. 87021 *Robert the Bruce* has just got the road to depart Glasgow Central on 30 September 1978. (S. Clark)

Class 303 unit No. 303014 is in the process of being repainted into blue and grey. One coach done, two to go. It is seen here at Glasgow Central, waiting to depart to Hamilton, on 30 September 1978. (S. Clark)

Platform 5 at Glasgow Central and No. 40042 fills the station with exhaust fumes on 31 March 1979. A DMU and EMU occupy adjacent platforms. (S. Clark)

With the author silhouetted on the platform taking the photo, No. 311104 arrives at Inverkip en route to Wemyss Bay in 1984. (A. Gibbs)

An extremely careworn No. 37191 is captured at Glasgow Queen Street station on 4 July 1983. (A. Gibbs)

Night-time at Glasgow Queen Street station and No. 47550 *University of Dundee,* complete with 'Highland Rail' logo, has recently arrived on 13 February 1986.

No mistaking what day this is. Edinburgh–Glasgow Push Pull Driving Brake Second Open (DBSO) No. SC9701 is on the stops at Glasgow Queen Street on 28 August 1979. Your journey maybe subject to delay or diversion! (A. Gibbs)

A rather grainy shot of No. 27101 on the stops at Glasgow Queen Street in 1980, having just arrived with the ECS forming 1N05, the 23.30 departure to Inverness. This train also conveyed sleeping cars and attached at Perth to a similar train from Edinburgh. (A. Gibbs)

Hidden behind the cloud of steam, 'Whistler' No. 40074 has recently arrived from Inverness on 28 October 1980. (A. Gibbs)

A Class 101 DMU, No. 40085, and No. 27102 are lined up at Glasgow Queen Street station on 28 October 1980. (A. Gibbs)

Another late-night shot at Glasgow Queen St as the shunter uncouples No. 40085 from its train on 28 October 1980. (A. Gibbs)

A typically grubby Class 37, No. 37108, waits to depart Glasgow Queen Street in 1984.

There's no-one to be seen at Glasgow Queen Street as No. 37027 rests in the platform on 8 October 1980.

At Greenfoot, on the outskirts of Glasgow, we find refurbished Class 101 Metro-Cammell DMU set No. 177 en route to Dunblane on 23 April 1979. (S. Clark)

No. 37199 clatters through the countryside at Greenfoot on 23 April 1979 with a very mixed freight that includes some TTA tanks, chemical tankers, Presflo and Cemflo cement wagons, plus bogie bolsters, mineral wagons and a former pipe wagon. (S. Clark)

With the light failing on 23 April 1979, an unidentified Class 26 is captured at Greenfoot with a short train of pipes. The brake vans lights glow in the gloom. (S. Clark)

Milngavie and a line-up of former blue trains. From left to right we have: Nos 303060, 303064 and 303014.

No. 303014 again, this time at Dalmuir on 7 October 1978. It looks like there is some major work going on here – notice that the cable drum has been left out on the platform. Ninety-one Class 303s were built and, along with the Class 311s, were synonymous with the Glasgow suburban network. (S. Clark)

Dalmuir station and No. 311110 approaches with a train bound for Airdrie on 7 October 1978. Outwardly similar to the Class 303s, units Nos 092 to 110 were built by Cravens rather than Pressed Steel. (S. Clark)

We move further up the line to Kilpatrick, where we find No. 303089 as part of a six-car working to Helensburgh Central on 7 October 1978. I think the guy sitting on the platform bench has probably outgrown riding a Chopper bike! (S. Clark)

No. 303039 departs Kilpatrick en route to Airdrie on 7 October 1978. Like the first generation DMUs, it was always a scramble to get the good seats right behind the driver's cab. (S. Clark)

I've always had a soft spot for the Class 26s and 27s. Being a southern man brought up with their bigger Class 33 cousins, it's no wonder. No. 27041 clatters through Kilpatrick station with an unidentified working on to the West Highland Line on 7 October 1978. (S. Clark)

Departing Dumbarton Central for Helensburgh Central on 7 October 1978 is No. 303014. The station is still sporting enamel signage. (S. Clark)

Also captured earlier in the day and now slowing for the station stop at Dumbarton Central, No. 27041 is working towards Glasgow Queens Street on 7 October 1978. (S. Clark)

The penultimate example of the class, No. 303091 brings up the rear of a service bound for Balloch on 7 October 1978. (S. Clark)

Another six-car Class 303 working, with unit No. 005 leading, arrives at Dumbarton Central en route to Airdrie on 7 October 1978. (S. Clark)

At Dalreoch, unit No. 303066 swings left towards Helensburgh on 7 October 1978. The line on the right leads to Balloch (Balloch Pier until 29 September 1986). (S. Clark)

No. 27040, sporting red buffer beam and silver-painted buffers, approaches Dalreoch with a train off the West Highland Line bound for Glasgow Queen Street on 7 October 1978. (S. Clark)

Balloch Pier station and a six-car Class 303 set waits to depart south on 26 July 1975. In the background the paddle steamer *Maid of the Loch* can be seen. The steamer services on Loch Lomond finished in August 1981 and the ship was left to rot. It has since been restored and hopes are high that she can be put back into working order again. (C. Parker)

Running along the banks of the Clyde at Craigendoran on 7 October 1978 is No. 27014, heading for Oban or Fort William. (S. Clark)

Helensburgh Central and units Nos 311102 and 303062, now sporting the blue and grey livery, can be seen on 7 October 1978. (S. Clark)

On to the West Highland Line and an unidentified Class 37 is captured at Garelochead. One image that didn't make the cut for the book was of the Chipmans weed-killing train at this location – too much deterioration of the slide.

Raining in the Highlands – whatever next. Large Logo-liveried No. 37408 *Lord Rannoch* waits to depart Crianlarich in October 1988. The Mk 1 TSO, No. M4485, is from a batch built in 1957 by the Birmingham RCW.

No. 37404 *Isle of Mull* is at Crianlarich Low Level on 29 May 1986 with a permanent way train, the only visible wagon being a 'Dogfish'.

No. 37011 at Oban on 4 June 1982. The attached wagon is TRL51332, a Class B tank wagon built in 1964.

With McCaig's Tower overseeing the town, No. 37014 waits to depart from Oban with the 16.05 departure of empty tanks for Mossend Yard on 22 June 1985.

No. 37401 *Mary Queen of Scots* and No. 104325, more commonly known as the 'Mexican Bean', reside in the sunshine at Oban station on 3 September 1987.

Nos 27111 and 27117 power through the Highlands at Glean Viaduct, just south of Bridge of Orchy, on the Horseshoe Curve, on 26 April 1975. The unidentified train has a downrated Mk 1 Pullman car as first vehicle and also includes a lot of first-class coaches and a Gresley buffet car. No. 27117 was later renumbered as 27211.

No. 37027 *Loch Eil* waits at Rannoch to pass a passenger service while working a train of Alcan PAA hoppers to the aluminium smelter at Fort William.

The crew climb aboard No. 27035 and its short train of Mk 1 coaches and a tank wagon at Fort William on 6 September 1976.

Stormy skies loom over Fort William and No. 37026 *Loch Awe* in 1984. The adjacent coach is Mk 1 BSOT SC9017.

Just three coaches, including a Mk 2 BFK, are a light load for this Class 27 departing Mallaig for Fort William.

No. 37011 waits to depart Mallaig with a train for Fort William in August 1983. It looks like there is still a proper buffet car at the rear of the train.

After finishing the western side of Scotland we now head over to the east coast and begin our journey through Edinburgh, Stirling, Perth and Dundee to Aberdeen.

Just over the border at Marshall Meadows, near Berwick-upon-Tweed, we find No. 47435 working 1S21, the 11.00 King's Cross to Edinburgh Waverley, on 29 August 1977.

Powering away from Dunbar station is Gateshead-allocated No. 47404. It is working the 10.40 Edinburgh Waverley to King's Cross service.

An unusual view of the eastern approach to Edinburgh Waverley as No. 47593 *Galloway Princess* arrives with the ECS from Craigentiny to form 1A89, the 14.30 departure to Aberdeen, on 24 April 1988.

Coasting into Edinburgh Waverley is No. 47041 working 2G54, the 12.21 from Dundee, on 17 August 1983.

No. 20205 drags a poorly No. 47486 into Edinburgh Waverley. The combination is working 1B32, the 12.00 from Aberdeen, on 20 February 1986.

Smoking Napier engines fill the air at a very wet Edinburgh Waverley. No. 55014 *The Duke of Wellington's Regiment* waits to depart for King's Cross with 1E20, the 15.00 departure, on 4 August 1977. This train was named 'The Silver Jubilee' in commemoration of Queen Elizabeth II's reign. (A. Gibbs)

A much brighter day at Edinburgh Waverley and an unidentified Class 47/4 and a Class 26 wait to depart.

No. 47711 *Greyfriars Bobby* waits to depart from Waverley station in 1984 with the second generation of Edinburgh to Glasgow push-pull services.

A week's holiday at Berwick-upon-Tweed saw me travelling into Scotland most days. My train home was usually 1E29, the 17.07 Edinburgh to Newcastle stopper. No. 55011 *The Royal Northumberland Fusiliers* waits to depart south from Edinburgh; a Mk 1 GUV forms the first vehicle of the train. This was the week after Penmanshiel Tunnel reopened, the week commencing 20 August 1979. (A. Gibbs)

With a cloud of exhaust, No. 40103 departs from a misty Edinburgh Waverley station with 1A28, the 11.00 to Aberdeen, on 1 October 1978. The North British Hotel looms over the station.

No. 27206 is working an Edinburgh to Glasgow train on 4 August 1977 and is waiting for the permanent way staff to clear the track at a very wet Edinburgh Waverley. (A. Gibbs)

No. 47578 is nearly at its journey's end while working 1S68, the 09.32 Nottingham to Edinburgh Waverley.

A light smattering of snow covers the track at Edinburgh Waverly as No. 47630 waits for its next duty on 24 February 1986. The cab must be cosy as the driver has the window wide open.

Push-pull loco No. 47703 *Saint Mungo* is now sporting Scotrail livery at Edinburgh Waverley in May 1989.

We find No. 47708 *Waverley* arriving at its namesake station on a working from Glasgow Queen Street on 17 August 1983.

Gateshead-allocated Class 47 No. 47409 approaches Waverley station with an unidentified working in 1979.

Our last view of Edinburgh Waverley has Haymarket-allocated No. 47206 arriving with an unidentified service on 16 May 1985.

Princes Street Gardens in Edinburgh and No. 40104 departs Waverley station with a service for Aberdeen in 1980. (A. Gibbs)

The Sulzer engine on No. 27004 is producing plenty of clag as it departs Edinburgh Waverley through Princes Street Gardens in 1980. The Scottish National Gallery is perched on top of the tunnel. (A. Gibbs)

No. 47709 *The Lord Provost* arrives at Haymarket station with a Glasgow to Edinburgh push-pull working on 27 February 1982.

No. 27204 brings up the rear on an Edinburgh Waverley to Glasgow Queen Street push-pull working on 24 September 1977. An unidentified Class 27/1 will be leading.

No. 40151 is captured at Haymarket Depot between duties on 24 September 1977.

Due to engineering work on the routes via Falkirk, the Edinburgh to Glasgow Queen Street push-pull services had, on this date (11 February 1978), been diverted via the Shotts route and into Glasgow Central station.

Falkirk Grahamston station and a three-car Class 107 departs, bound for Edinburgh Waverley.

Class 101 three-car unit No. 101309 is just south of Dalmeny on a local service for Edinburgh Waverley on 13 July 1983.

An unidentified Class 47/4 heads south off the Forth Bridge and through Dalmeny station on an unidentified service on 13 July 1983.

No. 26034 runs light engine through Dalmeny station having just crossed the Forth Bridge on 13 July 1983.

An ex-works No. 47517 *Andrew Carnegie*, only named earlier that month, works 1C65, the 07.45 Dundee to Poole cross-country service on 28 August 1986. The train, seen here at North Queensferry, will attach to 1O25, the 09.45 ex-Glasgow Central, at Carstairs.

A very careworn No. 25040 is at Plean Junction working the daily Larbert to Alloa freight on 2 September 1976. It is reversing back to Alloa Junction. The driver is leaning right out of the cab for the propelling move.

No. 27040 heads south at Plean Junction with a short local service from Dundee to Glasgow on 2 September 1976.

No. 40103, seen earlier in the book on a passenger working, is captured at Plean Junction between Stirling and Falkirk with a fully fitted freight train on 2 September 1976.

A pair of Rats – No. 25066 and an unidentified sister loco – depart from Stirling with a service from Inverness in 1977.

An unidentified Class 47/4 coasts southbound into Stirling station on a beautiful summer's day in June 1986.

A very neat and tidy Stirling station plays host to No. 47545 and an unidentified Inverness-bound service.

No. 47038 is in trouble on the outskirts of Perth as smoke billows out from the underside of the locomotive on 8 July 1977. (S. Clark)

In failing light, a pair of Class 122 DMU cars arrive at Perth. (A. Gibbs)

No. 27038 takes the route towards Dundee at Perth with a train of UKF fertiliser vans on 5 November 1981. (A. Gibbs)

With the coming of the HSTs on the East Coast Main Line, a new service to London was introduced: the 'Highland Chieftain'. The train is seen here at Perth on 4 July 1983 with power car No. 43062 leading. (A. Gibbs)

No. 47711 *Greyfriars Bobby* powers out of Perth with an evening Aberdeen to Glasgow Queens Street working on 5 July 1983. Spare Edinburgh to Glasgow push-pull DBSOs were used with rakes of Mk 2 coaches on some services to and from Aberdeen. One of the two Scottish Region Mk 2D TSOT micro buffet cars is the rear coach today. It's either SC6613 or SC6614. (A. Gibbs)

No. 47328 is ticking over in the sidings with a Speedlink freight service in July 1986. Wagons include some BBA steel flats, a pair of VBA vans and some PCA depressed centre hoppers.

Lots of berthed coaching stock at Perth as No. 08762 shunts a van off 1H05, the 07.06 Edinburgh Waverley to Inverness, in July 1986. The Mk 1 BG sports a non-standard wide white stripe.

No. 47045 heads south through Perth with a Freightliner train as a Class 08 shunts Carflats into the Motorail unloading dock in 1975. A Vauxhall Viva HC leads the light load of cars. A great selection of adverts adorns the billboards on the bridge.

Bright winter sunshine cascades through the station roof at Perth to illuminate No. 47546. It is working the southbound 'Clansman', 1M42, the 10.30 Inverness to London Euston, on 5 November 1981. (A. Gibbs)

No. 27041 clatters out of Perth station with a Speedlink train on 5 November 1981. The first vehicle is a Procor 80 car transporter. (A. Gibbs)

In bright winter sunshine, rounding the curve from Dundee, No. 47470 arrives at Perth with an Aberdeen to Glasgow Queen Street working on 5 November 1981. (A. Gibbs)

Shunting some parcels vans and a Travelling Post Office coach, No. 08753 is captured at Perth on 30 June 1981. An unidentified Class 27 can be seen in the station. The Dewar's whisky bonded warehouse can be seen in the background.

No. 47163 was one of two locomotives allocated to Stratford that received Union Jack paintwork for the Queen's Jubilee. Now allocated to Haymarket, it crosses the River Tay at Perth with an Aberdeen to Glasgow Queen Street service in September 1982.

Departing from Leuchars station on 2 September 1981, No. 27028 plods south with 1G64, the 12.40 Aberdeen to Edinburgh Waverley. A Class 101 DMU can be seen in the northbound platform.

Sweeping northwards on to the Tay Bridge at Wormit is 'Whistler' No. 40058 with an unidentified service on 4 August 1977. (S. Clark)

Coming off the Tay Bridge at Wormit, we find No. 47516 working an unidentified Aberdeen to King's Cross service on 4 August 1977. Keeping up the recent tradition in these series of books, a Reliant 3/25 or Regal is parked with the Gas Board vans. (S. Clark)

Climbing the ramp to the Tay Bridge, an unidentified Class 122 and Class 101 combination heads south from Dundee on 4 August 1977. (S. Clark)

With Dundee Airport in the background, No. 27014 nears its destination with a service from Glasgow Queen Street on 4 August 1977. It looks like a Renault garage resides in the building on the left. (S. Clark)

Seen earlier in the book, No. 47206 makes another appearance, this time at Dundee. The train is approaching the station from Glasgow with an unidentified service on 4 August 1977. (S. Clark)

With dark skies looming at Dundee, Nos 27033 and 26037 wait for their next turn of duty on 4 August 1977. A Class 08 shunter can be glimpsed in the distance. (S. Clark)

By now the wet weather has descended on Dundee as the driver checks No. 26037 on 4 August 1977. (S. Clark)

No. 27034 waits to depart from Dundee with an unidentified service for Glasgow Queen Street during the week commencing 26 August 1979. Dundee station was always a bit grim; the only shining light is the Travelers Fare Buffet sign! (A. Gibbs)

Nos 27034 and 47053 share the platform at Dundee station during the week commencing 26 August 1979. That might well be my bag on the platform – there were no small rucksacks back then. (A. Gibbs)

A glorious autumn day as No. 47716 *Duke of Edinburgh's Award* powers out of Dundee with an Aberdeen to Edinburgh Waverley service formed of a short Mk 3 push-pull set and Mk 2 DBSO on 24 September 1986.

Possibly the filthiest locomotive I've ever seen. No. 37205 makes plenty of clag as it accelerates its Freightliner service away from Dundee on 4 August 1977. (S. Clark)

Dundee MPD and we find No. 40181 resting between duties. (D. Burton)

The little Class 06 shunters are synonymous with the Dundee area and here we find No. 06006 on 4 August 1977. (S. Clark)

A great photo of the Aberdeen to Carstairs postal train, seen here at Stonehaven on 29 June 1979. The station is still sporting its totem signs.

Arriving at Aberdeen under the impressive signal gantry is No. 47145 working 1A25, the 09.35 from Glasgow Queen Street, on 7 February 1980.

A fitter with a hammer – it's not going to end well. No. 47270 receives some attention prior to departing for Edinburgh on 30 June 1981.

Dyce station and No. 47425 *Holbeck* waits to depart with 2A80, the 17.27 to Montrose. The set of Mk 2 air-conditioned coaches looks like it's been lifted off an overnight service for this short journey in 1986.

Taken from a passing train in grim weather. No. 25062 is seen at Keith, shunting a single Freightliner flat wagon loaded with bulk whisky tanks on 29 October 1980. (A. Gibbs)

Bowling along at Keith, we find an ex-works No. 47640 *University of Strathclyde* working 1A52, the 14.52 Inverness to Aberdeen, on 1 May 1986. The loco had only been named on 11 April. (G. Roose)

We now return south to the Highland mainline and thence northwards to Inverness, Kyle, Wick and Thurso.

Arriving at Pitlochry station, No. 40063 makes a fine sight working 1T35, the 12.15 Inverness to Glasgow Queen Street, on 1 June 1976.

Grimy Nos 26024 and 26022 double-head an Inverness-bound service at Pitlochry.

Accelerating away from Pitlochry, an unidentified Class 47/4 takes 1S59, 'The Clansman', into the Highlands.

No. 47641 *Fife Region* powers across Slochd viaduct with an unidentified service on 26 September 1989. The heather covers the hills in the background. The Class 47 had been one of the original WR 'namers' as D1672/ No. 47086 *Colossus*. (M. Hull)

I had a couple of nights at the station hotel in Inverness when it was still run by the railway and we got staff discount. After an early cooked breakfast, I was out to photograph some of the morning arrivals. This is 1S25, the 22.40 Euston to Inverness, arriving behind No. 47404 on 4 November 1981. (A. Gibbs)

Powering away from Inverness, No. 47472 heads south with 1M42, the 10.35 departure to Euston, 'The Clansman', on 4 November 1981. (A. Gibbs)

With Rose Street signal box centre stage, an unidentified Class 37 gets a train away for the Far North in August 1983. (S. Clark)

Nos 26022 and 26029 line up at Inverness with departures for the Far North on 27 June 1978. A couple of spotters compare notes. A nice line-up of 1970s motors can be seen on the left: a Mini Clubman, a Land Crab, a Granada and a Viva to name but a few. (S. Clark)

No. 47118 has recently arrived at Inverness with 1N15, the 09.55 from Aberdeen, on 15 August 1983. Swift work has the tail lamp already in place for the train's next working. (B. Watkins)

No. 47149 is captured, light engine, passing Rose Street signal box at Inverness in August 1983. (S. Clark)

No. 26014 is captured at Inverness with a service for the Far North. In the background a Class 120 Swindon cross-country DMU, still sporting a buffet car, can be glimpsed.

No. 26042 is stabled at Inverness Depot on 16 May 1983. One of the snow ploughs can just be seen in the background.

No. 47013 is on the stops at Inverness having worked in with a service from Glasgow on 24 August 1983.

A lot of southern interlopers at Inverness on 18 August 1987: an SR-allocated GUV and Stratford-allocated No. 47570 complete with cockney sparrow motif.

It's before 6.00 a.m. as the sun rises at Inverness. Newspapers and mail are being loaded aboard 2K03, the 06.15 departure to Wick and Thurso. The driver on No. 26105 gets a few minutes to read the fresh news. (A. Gibbs)

A wet day at Inverness and No. 26023 waits to depart with 2K08, the 10.35 service to Kyle of Lochalsh, on 29 July 1981.

A Class 120 Swindon cross-country DMU arrives at Inverness from Aberdeen on 27 June 1978. The destination blind already changed for the return journey. Unidentified members of Class 47 and 08 can also be seen. (S. Clark)

A grubby-looking No. 47635 *Jimmy Milne* waits to depart Inverness with 1T42, the 18.20 departure to Edinburgh, in August 1988.

On Inverness Depot on 29 October 1980 are Class 20s Nos 184 and 039. The yellow Renault 5 stands out against the dark background. (A. Gibbs)

No. 26042 pilots a poorly No. 37011 into Inverness with 2N12, the 07.10 from Kyle of Lochalsh, on 30 June 1982. Even with the dead Class 37, the short train shouldn't have been too much of a load for the Class 26.

It's a grey day at Dingwall as No. 26035 stops with 2K03, the 06.15 from Inverness to Wick and Thurso, on 29 October 1980. The station is a hive of activity with various Post Office vans picking up mail for the outlying villages. An old Gresley coach, now in Departmental use, sits in the bay platform. (A. Gibbs)

Another view of No. 26035 at Dingwall with the 06.15 from Inverness to Wick and Thurso on 29 October 1980. At least five Royal Mail vans, including a Morris Marina and Bedford HAs, can be seen. (A. Gibbs)

Curving into Dingwall from the Kyle of Lochalsh line is No. 26021 with 2N20, the 11.05 Kyle of Lochalsh to Inverness service, on 29 October 1980. (A. Gibbs)

No. 26021 has arrived at Garve on 29 October 1980 with 2K02, the 06.05 Inverness to Kyle of Lochalsh, and meets No. 26041 working 2N12, the 07.04 Kyle to Inverness. 2K02 was late this day, hence the photos at Dingwall of the later Wick train, which ran first from Inverness. (A. Gibbs)

Trains pass at Lairg. I'm behind No. 26015 on this cold morning, en route to Kyle of Lochalsh. The other Class 26 is unidentified. Waiting to pick up the mail is a Duple-bodied Bedford bus belonging to Sutherland Transport. (A. Gibbs)

Strathcarron station and an unidentified Class 26 pauses with an Inverness to Kyle of Lochalsh service. I'm not sure what the two guys walking down the track are doing.

A nice shot of No. 26042 near Plockton. The loco is working 2K14, the 17.55 Inverness to Kyle of Lochalsh, on 24 June 1982.

We find No. 26032 working four Mk 1 coaches forming 2K02, the 06.55 Inverness to Kyle of Lochalsh, near Plockton on 26 June 1982.

Bright sunlight illuminates No. 26021 at the end of the line, Kyle of Lochalsh, on 29 October 1980. It looks like there's more rain on the way. (A. Gibbs)

Another view of No. 26021 at Kyle of Lochalsh on 29 October 1980, running round its train. There's plenty of Royal Mail activity as post is unloaded from the train. Lots of period trucks and cars in the view too. (A. Gibbs)

A classic location for photographs. No. 26040 waits to depart from Kyle of Lochalsh with a service for Inverness in 1983. (P. Dalton)

Class 20s Nos 20126 and 20114 are at Invergordon on 28 May 1975 with a train of LPG tanks bound for the British Aluminium works there. The smelter closed, after just ten years of operation, in 1981.

A great view of Helmsdale station as No. 37419 pauses with 2H62, the 12.05 from Wick to Inverness, on 2 May 1986. (G. Roose)

No. 26035 powers away from Helmsdale station with a service from Inverness to Wick and Thurso. Four Mk 1 BGs form the front part of the train, showing how much mail and parcels traffic there used to be to such remote locations.

At Georgemas Junction trains to and from Inverness are detached from and attached to portions for Wick and Thurso. Here we find No. 37418 *An Comunn Gaidhealach* waiting to depart south from Wick, with No. 37416 bringing in the portion from Thurso, on 7 September 1987. (M. Darlow)

No. 37017, equipped with steam heat, is captured at Thurso with a service for Inverness on 22 June 1982. The Class 37s were great locos to have in the Highlands, taking over the sterling service given by the Class 26s and 27s. (M. McDermott)

At Thurso we find No. 37421 framed by the station's overall roof on 24 July 1988. (G. Roose)

Literally the end of the line for both this train and the book. No. 37414 makes a fine sight at Wick. The locomotive is waiting to depart with 2H62, the 11.22 to Inverness, on 24 July 1988. (G. Roose)